BILLY McCARTY, SR.

Ruby

BILLY McCARTY, SR.

Ruby

SPIRIT MOUNTAIN PRESS

ISBN - 0-910871-03-5

Interviewing and Editing:
Yvonne Yarber and Curt Madison

Photography:
Curt Madison (unless otherwise noted)

Koyukon Translations:
Eliza Jones

Material collected June 1980 and April 1982 in Ruby, Alaska

Manuscript approved by Billy McCarty Sr. May 1981 (except for Chapter Six which was approved by Clara Honea in 1982)

SPIRIT MOUNTAIN PRESS
P.O. BOX 1214 FAIRBANKS, ALASKA 99707

Produced And Funded By:
Yukon-Koyukuk School District of Alaska

Regional School Board:
Donald Honea Sr. - Chairman
Pat McCarty - Vice Chairman
Fred Lee Bifelt - Clerk
Eddie Bergman - Treasurer
Luke Titus

Superintendent: Joe Cooper
Assistant Superintendent: Fred Lau
Project Coordinator: Don Kratzer

Supplemental Funding:
Johnson O'Malley Grant - EOOC14202516

Library of Congress
Cataloging in Publication Data

Madison, Curt
Yarber, Yvonne
McCarty, Billy Sr. - Ruby. A Biography
YKSD Biography Series
ISBN 0-910871-03-5

1. McCarty, Billy Sr. 2. Koyukon-Athabaskan
3. Alaska Biography

Cover photo:
Billy McCarty Sr. in Ruby, Alaska. June 1980.

Frontispiece:
Front row, l-r: Esther McCarty, Deedee McCarty, Clara Honea, Don Honea holding adopted granddaughter Raelene, Morris McCarty, Glenn Honea; back row: Kandra holding son Allen McCarty Jr., Allen McCarty Sr., Billy McCarty Sr., Pat McCarty holding Alitha, Bill McCarty III "Willy", Wayne "Rocky" Honea, Melvin Captain, Jannis Captain, Billy Honea. 1981.

A Note From a Linguist

As you read through this autobiography you will notice a style and a diction you may not have seen before in print. This is because it is an oral storytelling style. This autobiography has been compiled from many hours of taped interviews. As you read you should listen for the sound of the spoken voice. While it has not been possible to show all the rhythms and nuances of the speaker's voice, much of the original style has been kept. If posssible you should read aloud and use your knowledge of the way the old people speak to recapture the style of the original.

This autobiography has been written in the original style for three reasons. First, the original style is a kind of dramatic poetry that depends on pacing, succinctness, and semantic indirectness for its narrative impact. The original diction is part and parcel of its message and the editors have kept that diction out of a deep respect for the person represented in this autobiography.

The second reason for keeping the original diction is that it gives a good example of some of the varied richness of the English language. English as it is spoken in many parts of the world and by many different people varies in style and the editors feel that it is important for you as a reader to know, understand and respect the wide resources of this variation in English.

The third reason for writing in the original style is that this style will be familiar to many of you who will read this book. The editors hope that you will enjoy reading something in a style that you may never have seen written before even though you have heard it spoken many times.

Ron Scollon
Alaska Native Language Center
University of Alaska
Fairbanks
1979

Acknowledgements

Our thanks to the many who have assisted in producing this book; Clara Honea was especially helpful when her father's handicaps required an extra pair of ears or eyes; Pat Pearlman and Mark Freshwaters provided lodging and logistical support; Ron Scollon again for his Note From a Linguist; Eliza Jones for her counseling, moral support and translations, courtesy of the Alaska Native Language Center in Fairbanks.

Appreciation also goes to the Manley Hot Springs Community School Committee for providing a place to work; Bob Maguire for imagining that this project could and should be done; Joe Cooper, Fred Lau and Mavis Brown for their administrative support; the Yukon-Koyukuk School District Regional Board who continues to support local curriculum; and our Manley friends whose extra efforts made a difference, Bea Hagen who typed transcripts, Cheryl DeHart who typed final manuscripts, Janis Carney and Liza Vernet who volunteered proofreading time.

And finally, thanks to Spirit Mountain Press: Larry Laraby, owner and chief headache man; Doug Miller, layout with an artistic flair; Eva Bee and her bear, who do much more than just typesetting.

Foreword

This book is the twelfth produced by the Yukon-Koyukuk School District in a series meant to provide cultural understanding of our own area and relevant role models for students. Too often Interior Alaska is ignored in books or mentioned only in conjunction with its mineral resources such as the gold rush or oil pipeline. We are gauged by what we are worth to Outside people. People living in the Interior certainly have been affected by those things but also by missionaries, wage labor, fur prices, celebrations, spring hunts, schools, technology, potlatches, and much more. For residents, Interior Alaska is all of those things people do together, whether in the woods, on the river, in the village or on Two Street. It's a rich and varied culture often glossed over in favor of things more easily written and understood.

This project was begun in 1977 by Bob Maguire. Representatives of Indian Education Parent Committees from each of Yukon-Koyukuk School District's eleven villages met in Fairbanks February of 1978 to choose two people from each village to write about. A variety of selection means were used—from school committees to village council elections. Despite the fact that most of the representatives were women, few women were chosen for the books. As the years passed, more women were added to give a more complete accounting of recent cultural changes.

It is our goal to provide a vehicle for people who live around us so they can describe the events of their lives in their own words. To be singled out as an individual as we have done in this series has not always been comfortable for the biographees, particularly for those who carry the strong Koyukon value of being humble. Talking about oneself has been a conflict overridden by the desire and overwhelming need to give young people some understanding of their own history in a form they have become accustomed to. A growing number of elders who can't read or write themselves think young people won't believe anything unless it's written in a book. This project attempts to give oral knowledge equal time in the schools.

As materials of this kind become more common, methods of gathering and presenting oral history get better. The most important ingredient is trust. After many hours of interview, people often relax to the point of saying some personal things they prefer left unpublished. After editing the tape transcripts we bring the rough draft manuscript back to the biographees to let them add or delete things before it becomes public. Too often those of us living in rural Alaska have been researched *on* or written *about* for an audience far away. This series is meant to bring information full round--from us back to us for our own uses.

Too many people in the Interior have felt ripped-off by journalists and bureaucrats. Hundreds pass through every year, all wanting information and many never to return. Occasionally their finished work may find its way back to the source only to flare emotions when people feel misrepresented. Perhaps a tight deadline or the lack of travel money may be the excuse for not returning for verification or approval. That is no consolation for the people who opened up and shared something of themselves and are left feeling betrayed. We work closely with the biographees to check facts and intentions. The books need to be intimate and daring but the last thing we want to do is make someone's life more difficult. We need to share information in a wholesome way. After all, we're all in this together.

Comments about the biographies, their use, corrections, questions, or anything else is welcome.

Curt Madison
Yvonne Yarber
December 10, 1982
Manley Hot Springs
Alaska 99756

Table of Contents

Introduction

Ruby began as a gold mining town in the early 1900's. Billy McCarty, Sr., half Irish and half Athabaskan grew up during a time of hard work, wild play and boom town growth. Many say that Billy Sr. was pretty rough and wild himself in his youth but matured into a hard working and dedicated family man. Blindness hit him in the 50's and dramatically changed his lifestyle of subsisting off the land. Even today as he approaches eighty years of age he longs for his eyesight so he can be in the woods again. Billy suffered a stroke a year after working on this book. It has left him partially paralyzed and under the care of Careage North in Fairbanks. If his recovery continues he looks forward to staying with one of his daughters in fish camp during the milder months of summer. Despite handicaps Billy continues to be good natured and a wonderful storyteller. Some of his stories are here, others are with the people who have visited "Old Man McCarty" and heard him tell a tale.

Curt Madison interviewing Billy McCarty, Sr. June 1980.

Glossary

babiche - rawhide cut into rope for lashing sleds and snowshoes.

bootlegger - a person who makes, transports or sells liquor illegally.

DDT - $(ClC_6H_4)_2$ $CHCCl_3$ dichloro-diphenyl-trichloro-ehane used as an insecticide. Rachel Carson's book *Silent Spring* explained the deadly aspects of DDT in the early 50's and led to its restriction. Her premise was that since DDT did not break down it gradually accumulated in the food chain poisoning everything. The publishing of *Silent Spring* is recognized as the beginning of the environmental movement.

Iditarod - founded in 1910 as a supply point for the Iditarod-Innoko mining district. Population of 700 in 1911 declined to one by 1940. The trail from Anchorage to Iditarod was resurrected in 1974 for the world famous Iditarod Trail Race continuing all the way to Nome.

Kokrines - a well known and large Native village founded many years before Ruby by a Russian trader. Kokrines is now abandoned except for an occasional winter trapper.

Lomen Reindeer Corporation - one of the four reorganizations of the Lomen family reindeer enterprises. By far the largest herd owners, they were often charged with unfair range practices and questionable business methods. Conflicts with them were an important factor in laws restricting reindeer ownership to Natives.

prohibition - a federal law which forbid the sale or manufacture of alcoholic beverages. This law was an amendment to the Constitution of the United States known as Article XVIII passed in 1919 and repealed by Article XXI in 1933.

roadhouse - anyplace along the trail a person could buy a meal and a place to sleep. Mail trails almost always had roadhouses every twenty miles. Quality varied tremendously with the most transient kind being tents. Yet however rustic, roadhouses allowed a man to walk hundreds of miles without worrying about accomodations or food right across Alaska.

Ruby - built on the lust for gold she began in 1911. For a few years the population was over a thousand but soon fell to under two hundred and stayed there. The big strikes were twenty to thirty miles back in the hills away from Ruby so most of the original population were transient miners or people who sold them things. Presently Ruby has a school, post office, general merchandise store, liquor store, air service, saw mill, Dineega Fuel Co., Ruby Roadhouse, and a handful of serious long distance dog mushers. Ruby is a popular name in Alaska. There are two places, twenty-two streams, and six gulches named Ruby.

St. Michael - established in 1833 as a Russian Fort, St. Michael has always been a transhipment point for Yukon River traffic. Present population is near 200.

Synrock Mary - wife of Charley Antisarlook the first Eskimo reindeer herder in Alaska in 1885. Charley and his two brothers died in a measles epidemic in 1900 leaving the herd to Mary. To escape theft and range fires she moved the herd from the Synrock River to Unalakleet.

Local Area

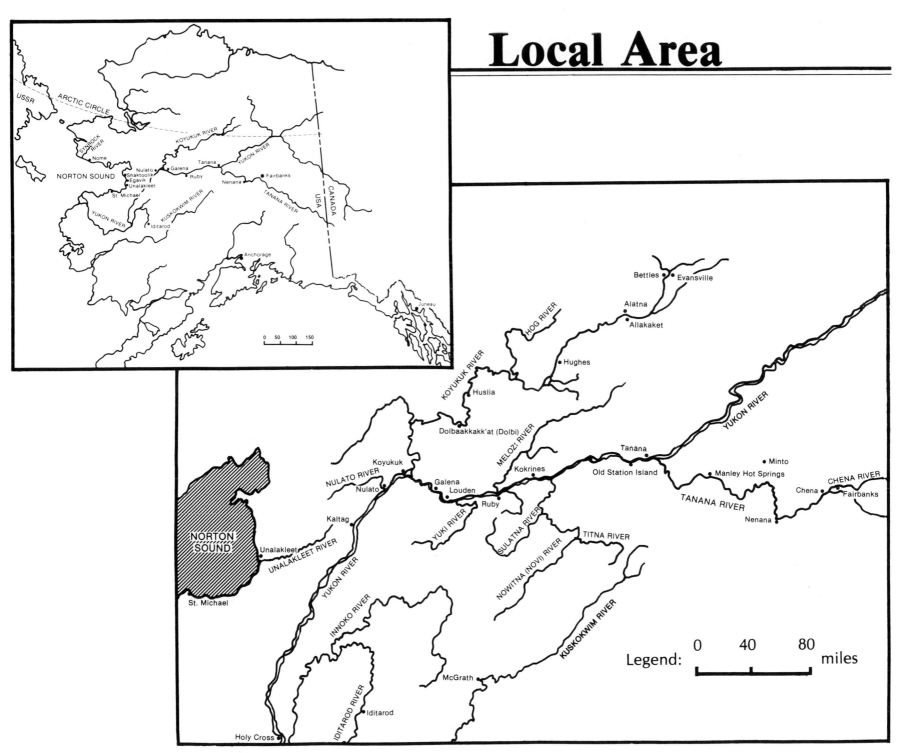

Chapter One: When I Was A Kid

Athabaskan and Irish Mick

I was born at Chena in 1904. My mother was a full Athabaskan woman. I had one brother, he died. My sister Madeline was adopted out when she got to be a year old. My father was an Irish Mick. His proper name was McCarthy, but I leave out the H. I had difficulty in writing it when I was a kid. I spelled it M-c-C-a-r-t-y, McCarty. He left me when I was a baby.

When I was about a year old, we started moving down from the mouth of the Chena Slough where the town was at that time. It moved up to where Fairbanks is now, the year I come down the river with my mother and Mc-Carty. We stopped at Tanana. He had a partner, that's what I was told. His name was Long Shorty.

When we got to Tanana, this Long Shorty robbed the Post Office. He's supposed to have got $1500 and left the money with McCarty. They caught Mc-Carty down the river at Louden, pretty near to Koyukuk. He wouldn't squeal on Long Shorty. He took the blame himself. I don't know where they had trials them days.

They started to ship him to prison on McNeil's Island. He jump out of the ship. They claim that the ship turned around out in the sea and they found him. He kept on swimming. They told him stop, or

"Bird's Eye View of Chena Alaska, July 30, 1905."

Photo by Robertson. Erskine Collection, University of Alaska Archives.

they'll have to shoot him down. And he wouldn't stop. They shot him right in the sea. I was real mad when I heard that story. I thought, doggone, if he was living yet, I'd murder him myself. He should have squealed on Long Shorty. He wasn't thinking of me.

School Days

My mother remarried to a fellow named Bill Dahlquist, and we got down to Kaltag. There, they fished and cut wood all summer for the steamboat. And he had two roadhouses. One, six miles below Kaltag and one sixteen miles below. That was the Iditarod Stampede Trail that time. It was in 1908 that I remember some parts of it.

Steamer Julia B. *at Chena, Alaska, circa 1905.*

The roadhouses were built out of logs. I remember there was about fourteen or sixteen beds on each side of that big long log building. The floor would be all covered with canvas. It was stampede over to Iditarod that year, 1908. All sorts of fellows coming through. Mostly on foot, some dragging their Yukon-sled. Some coming over with horses. And the mail team was loaded every trip with three or four passengers. The mail was run by dogs at that time. There was no such thing as airplanes yet. Just horses and dogs, that's all people depended on for transportation.

We had our garden on the Yukon. He planted a big garden at Six Mile Roadhouse. He fished too. He had five or seven dogs and he had to fish. He sold some fish to the stores too. At

13

that time mail carriers was buying a lot of fish, all the way up to Nenana, or to Nome. We stayed at those roadhouses for three or four years. Then the old man bought the roadhouse at Nulato off of a fellow called Ned Ragan. The old man stayed there until he died.

When I was a kid, I talked nothing but Indian. I didn't know one word of English. When I was about five my stepfather, the old man, taught me at home. I learned the English language from him in the roadhouse. He got books for me and everything. He learned me to figure arithmetic and reading, writing.

When we moved to Nulato, there was a lot of people living in those days. There's only a few of them alive right now. I remember I went to school for a while there. Fifty-five of us were going through, in one classroom. There are only four of us living now. The rest all died off with TB and pneumonia. They blame the stick dances for killing a good part of the Indians. They dance around a pole all night, and run outdoors in the winter, sweating. They catch pneumonia and died off. I went to those stick dances in Nulato but I never danced around the poles.

There was a Catholic mission at Nulato in those days. They had lot of different priests there. Lots of Natives say there was some good and some bad preachers amongst them. I remember Father Jetté and Father Rossi traveled up and down the river, preaching in the fish camps to the Natives. They helped them. Some Natives were needy, needy people. He got grub for them, Father

Photo by Clemons. Alaska Historical Library.

Mog'eau's Roadhouse at the head of Long Creek, Ruby, Alaska, 1912.

First Avenue, Iditarod, before the big fire. Circa 1910.

Iditarod 1911 by Clemons.

Johnson and Fornander's cabin, Long City, Alaska, the first in the Ruby mining district.
The photographer, Basil Clemons noted this as the place "where we voted August 15, 1912".

Rossi and Father Jetté. They were fine priests. But since they died, the preachers are no good at all now.

Joe Notti, fellow that was running the store at Nulato for A. J. Stockman told me, "The Catholic priests and all the Catholics made hypocrites or liars out of the people at Nulato. They were drinking and a fellow would come up and want credit. He even begged on his hands and knees and made the sign of the cross, and said, 'Sure, I'll pay you tomorrow,' Well, I let him have a little stuff and never saw that Indian again."

The Catholic Sisters, the nuns, taught school. They had a pretty good school down there. But I was just full of mischief. My old man taught me at home first. When I went into school, I got right into the second grade. I just started into fourth grade when I got kicked out of school.

Once the teacher made me stay in school to study my lessons after they send the kids all home. The teacher had a flower pot behind her desk, over her head. I got an idea. I emptied that pot of flowers and dirt. I emptied it out and filled it full of water. And I got a thread that I tied one end to the flower pot. I led the thread to my desk.

My desk was close to the teacher's desk. In the morning, we said our prayers. I was pious. Then, just as soon as we sit down

Nulato Mission third and fourth grades, 1914. Sitting back to front: Annaciata, Madeline Notti, Lilly Stickman, Fred Stickman. Row two: Priscilla Stickman, Olga Nicholi, Lucy Stickman, Julia Kriska, Antoinette George. Standing left to right: Johnny Warner, Esther McGinty, Willy McCarty (Billy Sr.), Edward Sipary, Theodore, Frank Ambrose.

for the Sister to teach us our lessons, I pulled a little bit on the string. I didn't pull it all the way, but water splashed over her head. She looks up and just that time I pulled the string hard. She got that full bath of all the water right on her face. One of the girls, Poldine Carlo's mother, squealed on me. It was lots of fun for me, but gee whiz, I realize nowadays that I did wrong.

The Superior said I needn't come to school anymore. I say, that's fine. I loved that. When I went home I told the old man I got kicked out of school. He said, "Well, as long as you can read and write pretty good, and figure. That's all you'll need in life anyway. I think you'd better go to work from here on." I started work. Eleven years old and I went to Unalakleet to work for the reindeer.

Lincoln Day 1914 at Nulato school. The second student standing to the right of the teacher's desk is "Willy" Billy McCarty Sr., Fred Stickman is to his left.

Reindeer Herding

A soldier, Sgt. Munson and Dr. Lamb were going to the fair at Shaktoolik. It was in the later part of the winter of 1916. Shaktoolik was forty miles above Unalakleet. My old man Dahlquist had me go over as their driver with his dogs. I was a good dog driver for a kid so I just went along with them. Doctor Lamb might have paid the old man something, but I never got nothing.

We got to the fair all right. They played roping deer and hitching up wild bull, all such things. In sled deer pulling, the Lapps won it. They hauled about 2,000 pounds of some rock. They played games at night. They had all kinds of races, foot races on the tundra without snowshoes. That's where I met the Laplanders.

While I was over there the Lapps started hiring. When they hired them young boys, ten dollars, I was beside myself. I didn't figure I'd get a job at all, but I tried for it. I figured the Eskimos look at me and thought, what kind of a crazy kid? That fellow is never going to make reindeer herder. Finally, this Lapp, Clemmison was his name, sized me up. He looked at me three or four times and finally he picked me up. I guess he thought I'd make a good reindeer herder. I stayed there three years. Never came back home once all those three years.

It turned out, in the winter months, just one fellow could handle one of those herds once he learned. I handled them alone even though I was a kid. They don't travel. It's reindeer country anyway. They're at home anywhere. We moved three times a year. Summer camp, and the fall and the winter.

In the daytime we'd have to circle around the herd and bunch them up a little. Then for about eight hours they'd be left alone. There was twenty-three or twenty-four thousand reindeer in Clemmison's herd that I worked in. The reindeer was at home. They didn't want to stampede or go run off.

Summer camp was on the coast. Soon as the sun got pretty hot, or when mosquitos or horseflies got thick, the reindeer would come to the sea. Gee whiz, you'd see for miles along the beach, nothing but horns. They'd stand all day in the water. Nothing but heads and horns. Falltime we'd go a little farther inland, and in wintertime go about thirty-five miles further, where there's thicker moss for feeding.

Winter camp we made sled deer out of any bulls. The first year I was there, I was afraid of some reindeer. In the fall of the year especially. They were bulling that time, in rut. I'd carry a pile full of gravel in my jumper pocket. When a bull gets close to me, looking for a fight, and I know I can't handle him, I just throw a little gravel

Reindeer fair, probably in Unalakleet.

on their horns. Then they shake their head and that takes the fight out of them.

After that first year I was ready for any bulls to come at me. I could handle them then. You got to know how to get a hold when they're coming up to you. You got to be quick. Twist them and throw them on their sides. They wouldn't come at you again. Once you'd throw them they're licked. They're a small animal. Caribou is a little larger. I noticed later when I herd reindeers at Kokrines, you could tell caribou in the herd because he'd be a head taller than the reindeer.

Being amongst those herders I picked up a little of their language, picked up some Eskimo too. People go from one herd to another to sort out their stray reindeer. They pick them out, rope them and take them back to their own herd.

I remember Synrock Mary, the Reindeer Queen, they call her. Between St. Michael and Unalakleet, she had a herd of reindeer. She was married to two men. They done whatever she bid. She sat in a rocking chair. She was short woman, but must have been five or six feet wide. She had a rope from the ceiling and a great big chair made especially for her. She let herself down easy on that rocking chair. And to get up, she gets a hold of that rope. She weighed over 300 pounds I guess.

We stayed at her place while we were at the

Herding reindeer at an unidentified location in Alaska.

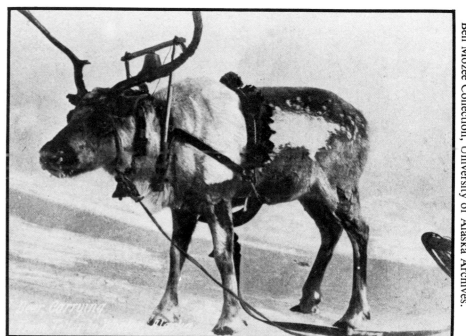

Sled deer carrying U.S. mail from Teller to Wales, Alaska.

herd, sorting out the reindeer. In the corner of her building there'd be a fifty gallon barrel, whiskey barrel of seal oil. Fresh seal oil. And on the lid of that barrel would be army cup, that holds a quart. Every morning we'd get up, each one of us would go over to the barrel and dip out and drink a cup of seal oil. Here it was kind of a religion with her. She says, "If you don't drink no seal oil, you'll never be a man." Well, before I left the coast, I was a regular Eskimo. I wanted seal meat and seal oil. But I couldn't drink the old rank stuff. It had to be fresh.

1918 Flu

There had been flu every spring around the Yukon. But 1918 was that big flu where it killed about 900 Eskimos. I was reindeer herding alone and tried to get into Unalakleet for supplies. Unalakleet was quarantined. I couldn't get into that town. Them guards they had head of the village were pretty strict. They saw me coming and they all come out in a body, some with picks, spears and clubs. They went after me. That whole body of men come after one little lone person. They told me to go back. I went back as far as Five Mile Cabin.

They kept everybody out of Unalakleet. They even left the mail out of town, five miles each way. They fumigated the mail. I gave them a note for groceries. The guards sent me whole load of groceries by the Lapps. Clemmet Clemmison was the one. His son is of the same name. That was before I got the flu. But not one person in Unalakleet got it. Twelve miles away they got it, and far

Reindeer roundup in a corral.

up as Nome. Egavik is where everyone had the flu.

I was back out herding deer alone when I got the flu. Peter Demoski and Slim Dick were herding with me, but they got quarantined at Unalakleet. I was twelve miles above there. I didn't feel no pain. I came home to summer camp and it took me long time to walk the three or four miles coming off the hills. I notice that I was resting. Every once in a while I sit down and rest. I had no ambition in me at all. Not even ambition to get up and walk. Several times there I was going to sleep. I said, "Get up, Bill. Don't fall here, out in the tundra, anywheres. Get up and go." I kept saying it to myself. And each time I got up, I'd walk a little farther, but I got tired.

Finally I got to my tent. I tied up my herding dog. I just barely made it to my sleeping bag. Our sleeping bags was made out of deerhide, with the fur inside. I got into that bag and dozed off. I was that way for ten days. Ten days in the sleeping bag. When I got up, gee, I was pretty dirty and sweat. I start looking around the table for something to eat. I saw some milk. I tried to punch a hole in that with a nail, but I could barely do it. I was that weak.

After I got so I could walk again, I went to Egavik. The village was about a half mile from where we were camping for the summer. I reached the river and could see across. The dogs were loose. They were eating on dead bodies. I saw people sitting at their doorstep that were dead. Babies were crying. Gee, I had to go over to save some of the children. But it was all I could do. I was still weak.

I had to swim across the river, small river. It was pretty near as big as Melozi River if you have been up there. When I got across, it was awful to see. Woman, boys and men all died. Some of them hanging. They saw their fellow man dying right off, so they hung themselves on this babiche made from seal skins. Two big boys, hanging down from the ceiling. The village was abandoned after that. They moved to Shaktoolik, or on the way. They tell me 900 Eskimos died that year.

Not long after that Lomen and Lindeberg over at Nome bought the Lapp's herd that I was working for, Clemmison's herd. They wanted me to stay on as a herder, but I got tired. I wanted to come home to Nulato.

Chapter Two: Jack Of All Trades

The Army

When I was thirteen or fourteen years old, still herding deer, I tried to enlist. Me and this Eskimo boy. "Let's join the army," I said. We sailed over to St. Michael in the winter, over in sled. There's glare ice along the coast and we had bone runners. We had a hole in the sail too for watch out where we look ahead of us for crack in the ice or open places. We had plenty wind and scooted over there in no time.

In St. Michael the officer said, "You look pretty young to enlist." I told him I was of age. He said, "Is your father and mother living?"

I says, "Yeah, my stepfather and my stepmother is living in Nulato." When I discovered that they'd sent a telegram to Bill Dahlquist at Nulato, gee, I got scared and beat it back to Unalakleet to herd reindeer some more. I didn't know that the old man would wire back to St. Michael that I was pretty small for my age, but was old enough for the army all right. I didn't know he would lie for me. I just got scared too fast and beat it. That's all my experience with the army. Except this last World War II, they sent me a 4F card. One of the worst cards that a fellow can ever receive. They said I had too large a family with my five children to go into the army.

Home to Nulato

Like I said, I went to Unalakleet to work for the reindeer when I was about eleven years old. I stayed with that three years and I've been working at everything since then. I'm what you call, a jack-of-all-trades and master of none.

When I got home, I felt elated on seeing my people I grew up with.

I was happy to be back. And, by golly, I was considered a tough boy because I started out working very early. There was about sixteen or seventeen boys there at Nulato. None of them would ever beat me at anything. We'd play hockey and football. I stayed there a while.

Then I went down to the mouth of the Yukon in the spring with a couple of fellows who was coming down the river. I fished for a while. Then I worked for Frank Kerns. He was getting the fish, he had a big boat, two engines. He had a Native cooking for him before that, but the Native quit. He asked me if I can cook. I say, "No, I never cooked before, but I can try at it." I got the job.

The way it was, I didn't have to cook very much anyway, just fried eggs, bacon or a potato or two. And we had breakfast and supper in

Marketing reindeer meat at Fort Gibbon (Tanana), Alaska, circa 1910.

the cannery, whenever we came in from our fish gathering trip. I was manual labor for him too. I had to count fish. I even delivered wood to the fish camp. I was about fourteen, it's 1919. I worked to the end of fishing season, little over a month. Frank Kern paid my fare up on the steamboat to Nulato.

I worked around the roadhouse, water carrier for the whole winter. I had long basket sled, about twenty-four gasoline cans and five dogs. I'd haul water till about two or three in the morning. The mail carriers wanted a lot of water, and the white people around town, the stores, post office, Marshal's office.

The Wireless Station, telegraph, needed a lot of water. I used a mule with a big tank. While I'm down at the river water-hole filling that tank up, this mule would turn back and just look at me. It's like he's laughing at me and saying, you think I'm going to haul all that water? He was a stubborn old mule. I'd whip him and wouldn't even budge. I forgot what I did to make him finally go. All of a sudden he ran and left me running behind. I had to run all the way back to the Station after him. And people all laughing at me. That's what hurt the most.

I told Jim Belcher, a worker there, what happened. He says, "Well, I'll fix that." He got a coal bucket and filled it with coal and a hot iron. He told me to stick that mule right in the rear end with the hot iron and he'll go everytime. Well, we had to get more water so I carried that on the sled. That mule got stubborn again and went in a pull-out where the snow was cleared. He wouldn't go. I took that iron, stick him in the rear, grabbed the sled and, doggone, he run right up the bank over to the road with me on the sled. I drove him back to the water-hole and had no more trouble with him. I had to do it just once. By golly, that mule was willing to go everytime I was ready to go.

From Sam Dubin to Tanana

In the spring I went up Koyukuk River ratting. Then I worked in a store for a Jew named Sam Dubin. I worked there over a year. He was pretty good trader. He had several stores up as far as Alatna, and on the way at Hughes, Hog River and *Dolbaakkaakk'at*. He moved the store down to Koyukuk Station. I helped in that store. He was going to set me up in business. But he married a young chicken from Koyukuk. That's what got me into trouble with him. Fooling around with his wife. He fired me. He was sorry afterwards. He wanted me back at Koyukuk. But I was at Tanana then. I stayed up there two, three years.

The way I got to Tanana was from working on the government boat. We got down to St. Michael and coming back I asked Captain Bergman if we could get off at Nulato or Koyukuk. He was a good friend of Bill Dahlquist, my stepfather. He talked with me and Larson Charlie and says, "If you boys stay on till we get to Tanana I'll get you a steady job." I decided to go to Tanana.

The captain got me a job at the Post as a woodcutter, a woodsawer with the steam engine. It was a crosscut circle saw that run by steam. We cut about 5,000 cords a year in the winter. Some days I'd have a good crew. Most of the soldiers were lazy bums anyway. But they'd pass wood and I'd do the sawing. We worked whenever we felt like it. Whenever we wanted to move the saw ahead a little ways, I went and got the horses from the stables nearby. And when it was snowing or too cold, I just kept the boilers. I watched the water so that it don't freeze in the boiler. Must have been 1920. Getting five dollars a day.

I was just fifteen years old when I first started sawing wood at the Post. It was an army post with soldiers. By golly, the first week some big soldiers tried to get rough and I handled them just like babies. I was tough. I'd been working before that all my life, and I was pretty skookum. I wrestled with them or I punch them up. Wrestling reindeer made me tough. I was known among the soldiers as One Punch Bill or One Punch McCarty. I never let a man beat me to anything. I fought in close if it's a big man and I put him out right away. They got to be my best friends after that.

Tanana was quite a different place in those days. The Post was pretty much all soldiers and White people. There was hardly any Natives. There was two or three, Andy Kokrine, Gregory Kokrine and Charlie Mayo, living among the White people. Most of the Native people lived up at the Mission, a little ways up the river from Tanana. That was where we'd go for amusement. We'd have dances and potlatches. They played music, fiddle and mandolin accompaniment and dance White man's dance. We danced the waltz, one-step, fox-trot, tango, square dancing and jig, sometimes Indian dance. My daughter told me nowadays all you have to do is stand in one place and wiggle your butt. But those dances came on after I went blind so I don't know how to dance now.

Frank Dufresne tagging beaver skins in Tanana. U.S. Bureau of Education boat in the background.

There was all kinds of business at Tanana. There was restaurants, hotels, poolrooms and stores. I had my meals at the Post, and even clothes. At that time the meals were cheap, a dollar a meal. But I played havoc with the Post women. Them officers and their wives would dance. They'd ask me all kinds of questions. They ask me if I dance at the Moose Hall. It was a big dance hall the lower end of town, high class place. I told then, "Oh, yes, whenever there's a dance you'll always see me on the floor." And they had one wild place there called the Greasy Spoon. I said, "I go to the Greasy Spoon, too, and we have lots of fun every Saturday night and fights." Those officer's wives don't like that. They'd say, "I think you'd better not dance with me anymore. You go to your Natives and go to the rough dance hall." They thought they were too high class for me.

I fixed them all right. On Sunday nights the officers and their wives all eat up in one of the two restaurants that was side by side. Well, I'd look through the window and see them all sitting around the table. Then I'd go pick out a homely looking Indian with a butcher knife stuck on his belt, and his manners is not good, and I'd order a beef steak. The tableware wasn't sharp and I know this Indian. He just acted in his custom, which is eating with a hunting knife attached to his belt. Well, he pulled out his knife, and takes the meat in his mouth and cuts off a big chunk to

Tanana Episcopal Mission church with the Yukon River beyond.

swallow. Some officers and their wives couldn't help but see him and they'd get sick.

One time I poured Tabasco sauce like it was catsup. My friend said to me, "I know that stuff, that's good stuff to eat meat with." I said, "Yeah, shake it lots, cover your meat up with it." Well he took a bite after that and rolled it in his mouth. He had to spit it out. It was strong stuff, the Tabasco sauce. Of course the ladies see that too. They finally talked to the Chinaman who was running the restaurant.

The Chinaman told me, "Whenever the officers and the wives are eating, don't bring no one in." Well, I said, "Our dollar is as good as theirs."

He says, "As long as the officers are eating, I'll give you and your friend a free meal." I took that. I was pretty bold. And I fix those ladies that way.

Then, once I went back to the Post gymnasium to dance. I was sitting around and the ladies come up to me. They wanted to dance. I says, "I thought you said I wasn't supposed to dance with you anymore." They said, "We forgive you." They saw I wasn't afraid of them and they're willing to dance with me after that.

Tanana with the N.C. Company. Corbusier cottage in the foreground. Circa 1910.

Whiskey and the Law

They had a lot of saloons, but this whiskey closed up about that time, prohibition, just before I came up. Even before prohibition the federal law was that a Native couldn't drink. The Native had to get his whiskey through bootleggers. Some White fellow would get their booze for them while they wait down the street. He'd deliver it wherever you specify. And the marshal was looking out for the bootleggers selling the Indians whiskey. There was a stiff sentence when they were caught.

Then when they cleaned up liquor during prohibition it got worse. The Whites and Natives all started to make home brew. They used barrels and put their ingredients in so many days till it's fermented good. Then we'd cook it and run it off. That's what killed lot of the Natives, fuel oil in that raw whiskey was poisonous. People were unclean with their distilling. I've made a lot of whiskey in my days too. When I first made booze I used a coal oil gasoline can and stick a lot of dough around it. Later years I got a copper still. That's when I made better whiskey. But it's hard to get that fuel oil out of the whiskey. We run it through charcoal, and bread and everything else we could think of. Still, there'd be some fuel oil in the bottle.

There at Tanana, Orville Webster was marshal then. I just went to a bootlegger and got two bottles of whiskey, two quarts. He had it wrapped up in newspaper. Just as I got out of his house, here comes Webster. It was getting dusk and there was a picket fence right there where I got out onto the street. He kept coming closer and I was trying to break those bottles over that fence. Doggone if I couldn't break them bottles.

Finally I took them and banged them right together. The glass was all over my feet and he come right to me with the gun in his hand. He said, "Stop that or I'll shoot."

I said, "Shoot and be damned." I wasn't afraid of nobody those days.

Webster says, "That's whiskey you got there."

I just pick up some glass and say, "I don't know what's in those bottles. Anyway, the evidence is gone."

All this time the bootlegger who sold me the whiskey had his door partly open. See, he's listening to us across the street. He said, "By golly you're a brave man to say shoot and be damned and keep breaking the bottles." He gave me two more bottles that night. Billy Carney was his name. He was an Irishman.

Once the marshal nabbed me on the Front Street. I was going down to the Post to get some soldering acid. I'd just got a bottle from someone at the N.C. Store and I lost the cork. I stopped at Vachon's, talking with him a while. I told him I lost the cork and asked if he had any caps. He gave me a cap to put over this bottle. I was going down the street with a light sweater and had it inside my shirt.

Webster was standing out there with a fellow by the name of Miller and nabbed me right as I was going by them. He said, "You got something in your shirt there." He reached over and started to pull it out.

I said, "Here, let me help you." I fumbled in my shirt getting it out and turned the bottle. I found I could pull that cap off easy. And there I

Town of Tanana from Fort Gibbon radio tower, 1911-1914.

was on the stone pavement in front of the jail. All the whiskey in that bottle was all spilled out on that pavement. But, gee whiz, I was all wet. My pants was all wet and the stone pavement was all wet. I said, ''When you first grabbed me, I got so scared that I peed in my pants.'' He couldn't arrest me that time because I ruined the evidence.

It was another occasion where I was delivering some white mule whiskey they was making at that time. In '22 or '23 this was. I collected the money and carried it up the Front Street. The boys that gave me the money all waited up there around the N.C. Well, I come out of a restaurant wth a gunny sack and this Marshal Webster saw me. He was a distance away but he was following me when I come out of there. I walked fast up to the N.C. and said, ''You boys get your bottle and take off right away so they can find the sack only.'' So each Native come up, snatch a bottle and went up toward the Mission. When Webster got there he picked up the gunny

A Tanana store, 1914. This fur display arranged by employee Ben Mozee was about $40,000 worth of marten, mink, silver, cross and red fox, lynx, ermine, otter and muskrat. At that time mink were only a couple dollars a piece and muskrats 25 cents.

sack but the evidence was all gone and he couldn't go after all of them. He said, "I'll get you some day." He never did get me though.

When the White people alone could drink and Natives were barred from the saloons it wasn't fair. I don't know the reason. That's when the White fellow would get their booze for them. Whiskey was cheap those days. Quart of whiskey was dollar and a half. A lot different from what it is now. I bought a bottle the other day for a friend of mine for eleven and a half. But there's a hell of a lot of difference between drinking nowadays and drinking in the 20's. Especially with the young people. There was whiskey around but they didn't drink it as much as this generation does.

I drank pretty heavy too. But I don't drink anymore. I can't drink with the young generation anymore. They're too rowdy for me. Everytime I drink with them they want to wrestle or fight. So I quit and made a bet with an Anchorage doctor. He told me, "Just as soon as you get out of this hospital you'll be drinking again." Not me. I quit for five years. I was a real alcoholic one time.

On the River

I sawed a lot of wood. One year, before 1923, me and two Roberts went thirty miles above Tanana to Morelock Creek, Robert "Pretty" Albert and Robert Alexander. We was getting Austin Joe birch wood. There was forty cords and we brought it all down on one raft. That raft was eighty feet long that we made. We drill the holes with auger and use dry poles for the pins, pin two logs together.

We had lots of trouble. We didn't have no power. We went up on a poling boat. The wood pile was a long way from the river. We built a slide, a chute down the hillside to the river edge. We used green poles and peeled them. We had to carry a bucket of water up the hill once in a while to wet this chute so the wood would slide down.

We didn't have no engine those days and used this poling boat to take the raft down. We got to the Mission and I was tying up to another raft which was high and dry on the beach. I never tie a moving object to something else tight. I had to slack it out. This eighty foot raft started dragging that other raft in the water and I had to play out the rope till I reached the end. Finally I had to let go. Next the raft came up to the mail carrier Ray Johnny's fishwheel. The raft just went against that fishwheel and smashed it close to the beach.

St. Michael.

I got off the raft and ran up to the Mission House and phoned down to Austin Joe at Tanana. I said, "You better be ready with your gas boat. The raft is coming. We can't stop it." Austin Joe went to work. He got three or four boats and they finally stopped the raft way below the towerhouse which was at the lower side of the creek. After the raft was tied up there's no more we could do. Ray Johnny never said nothing about his fishwheel we smashed. We're supposed to unload the raft but I and Pretty Albert went to work on a steamboat that next morning.

The *Seattle Number Three* was going down river to St. Michael. I worked on the boat for four or five summers. It was nice work but it was not enough pay. That's the summer we went on strike at St. Michael.

You must remember that everything was cheap those days. We worked cheap. We could buy a sack of flour for four dollars and right now it's about a hundred dollars for a hundred pounds. Still two and a half to three dollars a day and our keep was not enough pay. That's what we got.

Well, we were all working hard and thinking about better pay. It was the end of the season, getting cold and pretty soon the river would freeze up. We just finished unloading at St. Michael and seen four big barges loaded for us to take up the Yukon. This happened to be the last freight going up the Yukon this year. There was seventeen of us and they made me head of our strike, strike leader. We had our baggage all ready to go any second, suitcases, sacks, gunny sack or anything that held our stuff, our clothes.

The first mate, Fred Racey come into the place where we all slept. It was right after we seen those barges all loaded. We says, "We're on strike for five dollars a day and a dollar an hour overtime."

He says, "You won't get it."

Well, right then I says to the seventeen deck hands, "Let's go. Nothing to wait for." We were strung out on the dock and we put our belongings in the N.C. Warehouse at St. Michael. We all scattered out. Some to the villages and some playing pool. We weren't worried. If we had to we were going to go to Unalakleet

Photo by Clemons. Lulu Fairbanks Collection, University of Alaska Archives.

Steamer Sarah *on the Yukon River at Ruby, 1912.*

and come over the portage to the Yukon walking.

While I was playing pool I see Fred Racey coming. He said to me, "Gather up your crew and we'll go back to work. We'll have to pay it. We couldn't get no Eskimos since it's the last trip. They don't want to be caught up there on the Yukon too far away from their homes." Well, inside of five or ten minutes I had the whole crew back there and we all marched down to the boat. I went to the captain and asked him and Fred Racey if they were sure we're going to receive the five dollars a day and a dollar an hour overtime. They both verified it. We started work again.

We had all that freight to take to villages as far up as Ruby. On the way up the deck hands got off at their own village. All seventeen were Native boys. Only one of those seventeen is alive now besides me, Eugene Madros from Kaltag. And right below Holy Cross we went on strike again.

At the wood pile we refused to work or do anything there. We wanted dollar an hour for working on the wood pile. We got it too, dollar an hour straight through, Ruby to Tanana. And when we got to Ruby there was no deck hands left, just the three of us, Pretty Albert, me and Joe Benedict, who I picked up at St. Michael. He was an Eskimo boy who drowned at Tanana a number of years ago. He told me he lost all of his family, his uncles, mother, father, sisters, and brothers. They died in the 1918 flu. Anyway, in at Ruby there was business people all dressed in suit of clothes longshoring with us. They unloaded two of those barges with us.

Anyway, after the first strike that first mate and captain was still good to me. He didn't believe in having a grudge or anything. In fact, he treated me better. I was the only one in the whole bunch of deckhands that knew how to steamboat and do all the work. I was quick and fast. I worked on the steamboats about five seasons.

First Moose

I killed my first moose up at Tanana. At that time there was none up the Koyukuk, just bear and caribou. It was something for me to get a moose with an old fellow, Yaska. He was at a village there eighteen miles below Tanana. Old Station, they called it. I finally killed a moose towards evening. We skinned him and had to siwash out that night. It was just three or four miles to the camp but we didn't want to go back to the cabin. He's just roasting meat all night. That's when I found out the moose nose was good and tender soon as you kill it. You put it on a forked stick and roast it and butcher the moose while the nose is roasting.

I made a mistake there at the first moose I killed. Yaska told me to fold the moose hide three times so it would go in the basket sled. Well, I says, "I'm going to sleep in it tonight with the skin out and the hair inside. I had it wrapped around me and I was snug and warm. Along towards morning it got really cold and the fire went out. When Yaska got up to fix the fire he told me it was time to get up. I couldn't move. I got frozen in the skin. If he wasn't there I'd be left there yet. I couldn't get out. Big Yaska they call him. He rolled me closer to the fire and warmed up different parts. There I learned a lesson. I swore right there and then that I'd never do that again.

Tired of Tanana

All winter Cap Williams, Dave Williams was his name, wrote to me in Tanana to come to Ruby to herd reindeer. A friend of mine insisted that Cap write to me. He kept telling him I was a trained herder. Cap Williams started pay at fifty dollars a month. I just laughed at that. He finally agreed to $130 so I thought I'd try it for a while.

I moved to Kokrines to herd his reindeer. I was tired of Tanana. Anyway, I was running away, kind of. Too many of them women getting babies. I didn't want to get married yet at that time. So I went to Cap Williams' reindeer camp and lost contact with all telephones and women and everything. But then I run into the same trouble at Kokrines. I got married there.

Chapter Three:
Back To Kokrines, Married And Dogs

Working

In the spring, 1923, I came down to Kokrines from Tanana to work for Cap Williams herding reindeer. It was fun for me working closer to home and around my own people. But I didn't quite stay one year out there. Cap Williams was bossing me too much. I told him what's right but he seemed to have different ideas. He wanted his deer close-herded too much. I was all for letting them scatter out. Just round them up once a day. They wouldn't stampede then. If you keep them in a bunch the reindeer naturally think they were going somewhere. Eventually the caribou took a lot of the reindeer out of the herd and the wolves killed them off.

Cap Williams quit reindeer and sold out to a fellow from Seattle, Shorty Kells. Seems those fellows wanted me to work but they wouldn't pay me. I was experienced. I knew the business so I held out for $150 a month. That was big money those days.

Working herding on the coast I learned the Eskimo language. Their language is easier to talk than the Indian language. In Athabaskan you got to twist your tongue every which way. I was considered as a White man when I went through the different villages, but I could talk in Native just as fluently as other people.

Around Unalakleet I learned some Lapp language and my stepfather Bill Dahlquist was a Swede so I learned a few words in that Swede language too. Not to hard to learn those languages and pretty handy too.

When I quit herding I came to Ruby and people gave me different jobs. Like I said I was a jack-of-all-trades and a master of none. I made a trip up the Kantishna River to Lake Minchumina with a barge for Tom DeVane. And I worked for miners in Poorman. Eighty feet down the shaft and two tunnels

Photo by Father Jetté. Oregon Province Archives.

Kokrines, circa 1912.

at Danny Coyle's mine. Hard work but they fed good. Mrs. Coyle had everything on the table. Johnny Allen the dog driver from here was working there too.

Mining was the hardest work I ever did. My hands were all blistered. I couldn't work with gloves on. Picking my own dirt and wheelbarrow load. I had a battery lamp on my head. I had to fill up this wheelbarrow and bring it to the hoist. Then empty my load into the bucket all in so many minutes. Underground eighty to eighty-four feet. Ten hours a day. It got so that I couldn't get hold of a pick or shovel or wheelbarrow handles. My hand would be all busted up.

But like I say we lived good. We ate every six hours and the grub was good. I worked at the mines every winter from '23 to '28 for a month and a half each time. The other boys around here at Ruby worked two weeks or one week and they quit.

I tried a little of that mining. Jack-of-all-trades but master of none. Only thing I had was reindeer herding. I learned the whole thing in that line of work. Completely. I could make sausages, everything out of the reindeer. I learned as I worked with the Lapps. They lived the way they were accustomed and I learned all their ways of living.

Photo by Clemons. Alaska Historical Library.

Stroup and Labosky claim at Emil Bench, Long Creek, Ruby mining district 1912.

Jail

I was in jail once for four months. And they fed pretty good. Federal Building in Fairbanks. They fed us good and actually I wasn't in jail at all. I was made a trustee as soon as I got there. I could go around in the city but I couldn't go in any houses. Some places that I went into I made sure that nobody was looking at me.

I should never have gone to jail that time. I was framed by three boys from Kokrines. They were paddling down the Sulatna River and they wrecked up one White man's place. I got all the blame. They demolished the house and barrels and everything.

It looked pretty bad for me. The lawyer here named John Dunn told me to plead guilty and they'd give me a light sentence anyway. I did, but I swear that I'd get even with them fellows for framing me. When I got out I didn't have the heart to beat them up. I wasn't in jail anyway and I was treated pretty good.

Except at night. There was twenty-eight of us in the jail. We should have worn boxing gloves when we went to bed. Whenever there was an argument it would end up in a fight. Very little the guards could do about it because we was locked in jail already.

We sneaked some whiskey. I was to blame for that. Since I was made a trustee I could go out with the marshal or deputies to make a raid on people. I drove a truck. Load it and unload it. They had me put the whiskey and beer in a room right over our cell. I put a two gallon jug of homemade whiskey right next to the vent. We had one Native guy, tallest Indian in North America, came in just handy for us to reach up when the lights went out at ten o'clock. We pried up the grate and grabbed the whiskey.

I was trusted. They didn't do nothing to me about it. I knew the marshal well. I could tell him anything I wanted. Like when I got out of jail he gave me money to come home with. But I spent the money and then about a week after that he saw I was in town yet. By then I had a job with the FE Company right at the edge of town on Garden Island. I would start in a month.

The marshal sent a deputy guard around to the hotel and he brought me back over to the jail. He asked what I did with the money. "Oh yes, I spent it all," I said. "You give me some more and I'll get out of town." I was bold enough to tell him that.

Kokrines 1922.

He told me I could get in jail for obtaining money under false pretense. I think that's what he said to me.

"You'll go to jail too then because you got no business to give a prisoner money to go home on." I had him stuck. He didn't say nothing. Then he gave me some more money to go home but he made sure he paid my roadhouse bill first.

I was going to go down as far as Nenana that time and stay a week and head back to Fairbanks to work for FE Company. But I kept coming home. I was well liked by a lot of fellows. That's why I was made a trustee. And they gave me a light sentence for breaking in and destroying property. I would have got more but I had pull from everybody that was authority. I was well liked by Tom DeVane and the hotel manager and some White fellows around town. The marshal. They know that I didn't do this offense to this man's property but there was two against me.

That's the only time I ever been in jail. The old man thought I would be a jailbird before I was 21. He said if I ever went to jail he wouldn't give me nothing. When I got to be 21 in Tanana he sent me bunch of gifts and a hundred dollars. He kept his word. I had lots of opportunities to go to jail, but I'd always beat the case. I was one of those fellows that speak up for themselves.

Serum Run

1924 in the summer I fished with Dago Kid and Altona. They had boarding dogs that summer. Lots of dogs. I cooked dog feed, get fish out of the box, and take care of the wheels. When the water is dropping I push them out and when it's rising I

push them in a little. I went to the nearest wheels by five o'clock. I put those fish on the cutting raft and have breakfast. Then I go to the farthest wheels. By the time I get back the first batch is cut and I pack them into the smokehouse.

I got along fine with Dago Kid. He gave me a lot of privileges with his dogs. He had thirty-one or forty of his own. And that's why in 1925 I hauled the diptheria serum down from Ruby to Whiskey Creek. I'm sure you heard a lot about that run to try to beat the epidemic in Nome. Only a few of us still alive that took part in that.

I asked Dago Kid, "Why don't you take that job?" But he was too old then. He couldn't drive dogs anymore. And especially night driving. He had me run his dogs. It was pitch dark. Several times I stopped with my flashlight to see if the leader was on the trail. Hard all over. Windswept. I had to make sure I didn't miss the trail, but he was right on. Darn good leader, Prince. I had the pick out of thirty or forty dogs and I made one of the best times in the whole run, but I never said nothing about it.

Married in Kokrines

It was a pretty good wedding. I got married to her in Ruby. Laughable, I had to go up in Tom DeVane's big gas boat to pick her up. Two trips. First time her parents had to sign the release paper but I couldn't get them to sign. I came back down and went up again later. That time they signed the paper for me to go ahead and marry her. We courted each other for about a year.

44

I had the privilege of getting married before that but I wouldn't do it. I waited and saw a poor girl of a poor family and married her instead. I could have married school teachers. White women, but I thought I'd marry a poor girl and give her a home. And I did the right thing. We lived for forty-two years together until she died of cancer. I'm a very emotional man. It's pretty hard for me to talk about this. She was a darn good woman. Took me years to find a girl like that.

She was Athabaskan. Going to school in Kokrines when we met. Raised all my kids. She even wanted to work with me out on the trapline. I had them out with me one year but then thought it better to leave the family in Kokrines. Kids had to have schooling so I couldn't take them up every year. And I'd have to have a bigger boat. The things we needed in life out in the woods was so enormous. So I left them in Kokrines. I built a great big house, biggest house in Kokrines. Thirty feet by twenty-two feet. One story building but there was all partitioned rooms. Kitchen, front living room, and bedrooms.

Everybody that travelled up that way, some of them didn't even stay in the roadhouse. They said they'd spend the night with us. We fed better and no man ever left my house hungry. I had something for everybody all the time.

You can ask anyone along the river they'd say she was a good woman. I never quarreled with her. I had no reason to ever quarrel with her. She took care of the kids when I'm away. The money parts, she handled well. She took care of a lot of my business. She wanted to go even wood cutting with me, just to cook for me, but I wouldn't have it. She goes in the woods she's doing as much work as I do. Whether I want her to work or not, she just dive right in and work.

She was an honest woman. She took care of people's money and other things that needed taking care of. She handled all the orders and she was a good cook. She had a good table all the time. You can verify that from her daughters down at Galena or Ruby or Tanana or elsewhere.

We treated our kids well. Makes me proud to say that. They had lots to eat, clothes to wear, even money. I had every one of them get married as soon as they were of age. Daughters are all married and the boys except Morris.

After I got married I worked for myself mostly. Self-employed. Trapping, cutting wood, fishing. I hardly worked for wages at all since I got married. We boarded dogs at our fish camp. One summer we had 120 dogs. Gee, there was lots of noise up there in the evening when meal comes on. I cooked in drums. No problem for me when I was young. Work didn't bother me. Later on, my son-in-law, Don Honea, really helped me. I had everybody's dogs from here and some from outside town, Galena and along the river. I remember Bill Carlo's dogs got so used to going to my camp they just walk aboard the boat by themselves. When I delivered them back in the fall, I never tied a dog up. Just let them run home.

And we sold all kinds of fish. All we could do to fill the orders for salmon strips, salmon bellies, sides and dog feed. Compared to now it was a cheap price. Most we got was twenty-five cents a pound for dry dog feed. Now they get a dollar to dollar fifty. And strips are eight dollars. We used to sell them for dollar twenty-five a pound.

My wife was a number one fish cutter. Not as fast as Altona but Altona is too damn fast. Sometimes she cuts the skin and the fish fall off the rack. My wife was never in a hurry so she

Clara Honea Collection.

Tony Lewis, Billy McCarty Sr. and his wife Marie. Taken in Ruby a year after Billy went blind.

Clara Honea Collection.

Billy Sr. and his wife Marie during one of their last years at camp, 1966. Billy holds grandson Roger.

cut real good. I cut with her and I cut fair but not the best. I'm slow, but I still cut over fifty an hour.

In the summer blueberries were right close to us. We picked salmon-berries in early summer and blueberries after fourth of July when they're ripe. We picked rose bud berries and currants and cranberries. Some years the blueberries wouldn't be thick but some years it would be a heavy crop.

We'd store the berries in barrels and can some. I ordered a thousand cans from Sears and Roebuck and a sealer and pressure cooker. Towards the end I discarded the pressure cooker because it was too slow. We had to have a big cooker, so I made one out of a fifty-five gallon drum. I could cook several hundred cans at a time in it. We just put the cans in and filled it up with water. I made a lid to hold the cans down under the water and cooked them outside over an open fire.

The kids helped me considerably. They get in wood, pack water, and take care of dogs. All the things we have to do in life. Nowadays you can talk to any one of them and they'd say they had a great life. I don't talk to them much but from time to time when they were growing up I would tell them something that would be useful in their life. So that when they go on their own, they know what to do for themselves.

The kids wanted to do a little of everything. Some wanted to go trapping, some wanted to come along cutting wood. But you can't tell that to kids nowadays. I think our government is at fault on that. Especially with the girls. The government gives them a pension for every kid they have. I myself had some trouble on that.

I've been wanting another mate, but I'll be darned if I can get one. Because the government gives that woman some aid or something she depends on the government money. She couldn't marry a fellow if you asked them to be your wife. There's some old timers that are willing to marry a fellow but not for long.

Living is different altogether than life thirty-five or forty years ago. Everything is changed. We old fellows, we can notice the change in the world. I just can't cope. Especially when I went blind. Things happened after I went blind that never happened before and more things happening everyday. I just can't keep up with the trend of life. And drinking. They got nothing else to do but drink. In the early days there was no drinking amongst the people. Very little drinking compared with nowadays.

Kokrines school which was torn down 1958 or '59.

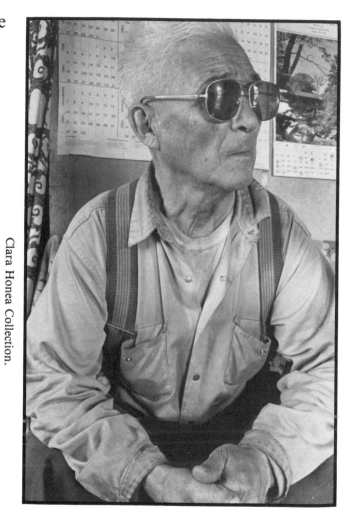

Clara Honea Collection.

N. C. Store

In 1947 they got me to be the head of the N. C. Store in Kokrines. When I took over the price of fur was high and we hardly had any stock for trading. Right away I got in a lot of stuff from Manley Hot Springs, Tanana and McGrath. Most of the stuff came by Lon Brennan and his son Lloyd from Hot Springs.

I carried all kinds of general merchandise but I wouldn't handle no liquor. They wanted me to, but I was chief of the tribe and council. One thing and another. I didn't want no whiskey sold at the N. C. Store. I just as well had. When I gave each customer their money for fur they'd come down to Ruby and spend it anyhow. And then go back up there wanting cigarettes and stuff on credit.

It's the only store I know of where all the people paid their bills. I was the only one with an outstanding bill and I paid it up here in Ruby.

I was a trapper myself and I know what the fellows have to have out in the woods for a stay of two or three months at a time. The N. C. Company had its home offices in Fairbanks. They directed me not to give a married couple over seventy-five dollars credit. But I used my own judgement. People got as high as eight or nine hundred dollars. I know all them people and I know their ability to work and pay. They gripe to me from Fairbanks. Young clerks in the office. They didn't know that the people have to go out long ways. They have to have a big bunch of grub and everything. But when they come in they all walk over to the store and pay up their bills. They all paid willingly. They were all honest people.

Eventually that store closed but Kokrines was still a thriving village. The stores in Ruby couldn't stay in business without the Kokrines people. They had their furs, lots of fur and they kept the stores up.

Carnival

Christmas, New Year's, 17th of March, Spring Carnival, they're a lot alike. Dancing, potlatching. Dog races for everybody. One time I came in in March from the trapline. Everybody was out after beaver. Five of us got in a poker game. One woman, Gladys Nicholi, two councilmen, somebody else and me.

Those two councilmen asked what we're going to have here in April. I was chief at the time. Right there I said, "If you want I'll send a message through Tundra Topics on the radio notifying everybody what kind of time we're going to have. That way everybody out trapping could hear about it." People as far away as Nulato, Kaltag, Coskaket, and Rampart used to come for a carnival. Kokrines was famous for potlatches.

I used part Native in that message. "I don't know what *nilaana* means," the announcer said, "but I have an idea." I said the name for moosemeat. That's the only thing that was against the law. "Save all your *nilaana,* you fellows. We're going to have a big time in April when we all come in." By golly, right that morning we took up a hundred dollars apiece from the five of us, including that woman. Five hundred dollars we raised in less than a minute. We got the rest from the trappers and all of us had a good time that spring.

Red Dog Gambling

Another time a bunch of people got together and started playing Red Dog. I was hauling dry wood for the house that time so I wasn't playing. Junk game. People bet on their sleds, dog teams, grub, some even bet their clothes. It's a card game. You hold so many cards in your hand. If you can beat the card the dealer turns over you win whatever is in the pot. They came to wake me up to settle up the game.

I went over to the gambling house and as soon as I got in they told me everything was in the pot and everybody went broke. Only my uncle had any money left. He had four dollars and he was going to take the whole pot with that four dollars. Several thousand dollars worth of merchandise in there. And Moses was sitting on the floor naked except for his shorts. All of his clothes were already bet and lost. I said, "What'll you give me to settle up your game?" My uncle says, "Anything you want."

I looked in the corner and there was a brand new pair of snowshoes, trail shoes. I needed some trail shoes so bad that time. "You give me these trail shoes and I'll settle your game right now." "Go ahead," they told me. My uncle didn't like it. They were his snowshoes. But finally he said alright.

"Everybody, each one of you, take back whatever you lost and start over again." That's all I told them. They made a scramble for the pot and took out their belongings. And I'll be darned if they would start over again. They learned their lesson from playing Red Dog that time. Right today I never seen Red Dog played anywhere. It requires a lot of money and people can lose all their belongings. That was about forty years ago.

51

Chapter Four: Trapping

Up the Novi

I had the dogs but I don't believe in racing with dogs. I had good teams several times. They always took me where I wanted to go. Distance didn't matter at all. When I was trapping up the mouth of the Sulatna a hundred miles from Kokrines, I went there in one day. Even with lots of snow on the trail. I couldn't even walk ahead of the team to break trail. They catch up to me and trample on my snowshoes all the time. I just changed leaders around every so often. I had a bunch of leaders. They'd plough through the snow for an hour or hour and a half, and then I'd put in another leader.

Trapping was good some years and bad others. Whenever the price was high we made good money. First I trapped at the mouth of the Novi for four or five years, then I went up to Sulatna, up toward the head of the Novi. There I had all I could do. Twelve lines. I caught a lot of fur. Outside of another Native, Frank Albert, I caught the most.

I covered the whole Sulatna and all its tribuatries. Took me nine days to cover my trapline one way. It's sure nice when you're getting lots of fur. Your pack gets heavy but you don't mind it. Especially if the prices were high. We were happy all the time.

When I moved from the mouth of the Novi I had to buy my new trapline. I bought it from a White guy, Joe Stoby. Paid him $200. He had just a short line up the river, but when I trapped I covered the whole river and a little on the Kuskokwim side too. But the last couple years the lines were a little too long for me. I was getting all in. I had to cut down part of my line. Twenty-two years I was up there. That will play a fellow out pretty fast. Going out everyday.

The Carlo boys were trapping up another river. They'd come over the head of Sulatna down a little ways and back over to their country again. They never bothered me. If somebody trapped on your line you wouldn't like it but there was no law against it. Fellow could set a trap three feet alongside of my traps. I can't say nothing. But we respected each other's traplines. It was unwritten law. Some White people got into fights over that, but I went so far up the Novi I was trapping alone up there. I had a large country. Covered the whole river.

Darn few fellows make trouble for each other. We generally help each other out. Like if we're freighting our outfit up river in a gas boat we take the other guy's outfit to his place and drop it off. For me an outfit cost around two thousand dollars for gas and everything. Then I generally have enough left up there for next year at least in the grub line.

I built some good caches. Bear proof. Wolverine or squirrels never bothered my stuff. I peeled all my cache poles and I built them high. On top of each platform I built a house. Fourteen feet off the ground. The house was about ten by twelve inside.

For grub I'd get a couple wheels of cheese, granulated potatoes and everything that wouldn't be hurt by freezing. We got powdered milk, onions, dehydrated peas and beans, corn, and dried eggs. Very seldom we used store eggs, fresh eggs. Only at home camp where we have a big cellar. We get a few fresh

Clara Honea Collection.

Billy McCarty Sr., Don Honea and daughter Tudy, 1950.

potatoes and eggs for that cellar because they wouldn't freeze in there. Right now that much grub we got for two thousand would be around seven or eight thousand.

We had all wool clothes. Heavy underwear and heavy shirts. Our good parka out of blue drill or khaki cloth. After the trail is broke I might drive nine or ten dogs at a time.

Trouble on the trail mostly came from rain. It's closer to Anchorage there. We have rain when it's snowing on the Yukon. And sometimes we'd break through the river. We get out of it but our sled and stuff gets all wet. It's a tough river to travel on. Gravel bottom and it opens up. Where you go one day, the next day if it happens to be cloudy, the ice will thaw. We had to be on the alert all the time.

Other trappers had trouble with bears, especially brown bears, but I didn't. I fixed up a trap out of poles and spikes and at home camp I use barb wire fencing. I take the windows out every spring and put them in the cache and string that wire over the hole. When Mr. Bear comes he sticks his head through that wire. They leave a lot of hair until the bear gets hurt around the neck. Sometimes pretty badly hurt. Then they won't bother barbed wire anymore.

Clara Honea Collection.

Don Honea where he trapped with a friend on the Dulbi River, 1958.

54

There's nothing left up there right now. All my stoves, gas lamps, beds, are all spoiled now. The cabins are down. I had nine cabins and 750 traps all sizes. That alone comes into money. Right now they're high. I got them while they were cheap. A dollar for big wolf traps.

When I went out in the fall I hunt moose on the way up and I stay out till spring. Sometimes I come in at Christmas but sometimes only my partner comes in if it's too far for both of us to leave.

My family stayed at Kokrines going to school. So I had to get an outfit for the winter for them too. Or if I didn't they could get anything they wanted at the store. My credit was good because I always paid up. I remember once I was in debt to Tom DeVane alone for $7,000. I owed three stores, N. C. Store, Carl Bohn and Tom DeVane.

I was sitting out in front of his store on a bench and he was inside typing some letters. He saw me sitting out there for a long time and I was kind of worried. I didn't know what I would do that winter. I was too ashamed to ask for more credit. Finally he came to the doorway and looked at me awhile. He asked, "What you going to do this winter, Bill?"

"I'm going trapping." I didn't want to give up. "I'll go trapping the hard way. I'll even line my boats up if I have to. With the considerable amount I owe you, I haven't the place to ask you for another outfit." He thought a while. Then he said, "You make out a list. Engines and everything you need." My credit was that good.

That was the year I moved up to Sulatna. I had been trapping at the mouth of the Novi, but I cleaned out that country until I couldn't get two mink. Beaver were all trapped out. And mink, marten, fox, otter.

That winter I paid off my whole bill and made enough to get through the summer. A kid, Merle Marie, went with me. He was only sixteen years old but he could do everything out there on the trapline. If his sleigh broke down on the trail he'd stop right there and fix it. If he broke his snowshoe or something, he'd tie it up that night. He never went to school. He doesn't know how to read. His father, Tom Marie, kept him home working down here at the Yukikaket. He learned everything from his father. How to tan mooseskin, fix snowshoes and sleighs. He could get a natural crooked birch, hew one side and fasten it some way to the side of his runner and make it to the next camp. That boy never got stuck.

We had only two hundred fifty traps but Merle made a lot of deadfalls too. He can't read at all so to pass the time at night he'd whittle the triggers for figure fours. He made them out of a straight stick a foot long or less. And he'd notch into another piece that holds the logs up, the timber. He drove a couple sticks in the snow and then lay one log down on the ground. A heavy log three or four feet long. The dropper would be six inches or so above that. Soon as the marten comes along he sees the bait on the end of this stick, the stick that's holding the upright up. He'd chew away on that and the first thing you know he's caught around the belly so he can't wriggle out. We had lots of those sets.

I've had a dozen or more different boys go with me. I tell them I'll pay them and I furnish the grub, dogs, dog feed, everything. They're more than glad to go with me. They even fought over it once. Bob and Nelson McQueston, two brothers. Oh, did they fight. 'Cause I pay them one-third of all the catch.

Don Honea skinning a beaver, about 1958.

It didn't cost them a thing. It was just their tobacco I wouldn't buy. They were more than glad to go with me and I never had a written agreement with any of them. I just paid them off as I had said. Verbal agreement. That's all.

I had my son-in-law, Donald Honea, go with me two years and another son-in-law, Bill Captain, one year. That's the last year I was up there. If I hadn't gone blind in '56, he'd still be with me and he'd clean the country out. He was always talking about "Let's clean up." That fall when he saw those marten track did his eyes ever bulge out.

"How many marten we going to catch?" he asked.

"Well," I said, "It depends on how busy we get. Maybe a thousand." He couldn't believe it. But he believed it that winter when we got a big pile of furs. Three hundred ninety is the most I could catch. I could do better some winters if I could get up to the head soon enough. The river was so swift that it didn't freeze up and there's canyons up there. I couldn't go around them. I had to wait until freeze up or build bridges out of trees and poles. Cross over on top of these bridges. It'd be way after Christmas when we'd get up to the real marten country, the head forks.

We didn't get quite three hundred the year with Bill Captain. We had difficulty getting up to the marten country and I cut the line shorter. I couldn't go as far as I used to. He was willing to go around those lines. Two side lines from each cabin and straight through on the trail. If I didn't cut him off he'd run both side lines and make me lose a day. He was young and fresh. Me, I was getting tired out.

We never made as much as we did the first three or four years. Fur prices were high. We got $125 a pelt for the marten.

I paid off Tom DeVane and Merle had so much money when he came to Kokrines he bought a suit of clothes for all the boys and girls. And mouth organs. He was buying everything in big lots.

Wintertime Water

I fell in water once. That's the day I was reckless. I was running down a moose and the moose crossed over the river above me. So I crossed. And my own fault, gee whiz, I started to jump. . . the river was open one place here in midwinter. I thought that I could jump across. I did make it all right but in jumping across I landed on the other side and that ice broke with me. Pretty near that current took me under. I managed to get out. Some streams like that with gravel bottom open up whenever it gets cloudy weather.

All wet I kept running up the bank and cross over a portage. I got the moose. I wasn't a fast runner but I was pretty good. I skinned the moose and dried myself up right there. I always keep my matches in a metal case. We can't tell when we're going to fall in and we want the matches dry.

I learned a lot of tricks from different Natives. Hunting. Like they told me never to drink overflow water. It'll play you out in a few seconds. You can put some twigs or spruce boughs in a hole with overflow then sip the water out, but you got to eat something with it. Piece of dry fish or cold pancake. If you're traveling and you drink it without eating you just fatigue. You can't move. I've seen White fellows, they wouldn't pay no attention to me. They'd drink water anyhow and, darn them fellows, they're just helpless after that. I never drink out of the overflow since the first Indian told me not to drink it.

Or if I'm hunting in the hills I kill a spruce chicken and eat the guts. You tear it open at the belly and swallow the green part of the guts. That's another thing that revives a fellow right now. Many times I was on the trapline coming home hungry or thirsty. I kill a chicken and swallow the guts. Boy, I feel fresh again. Not many of this younger generation know that. I guess some do.

Coming Down in the Spring

We built it ourself by watching how other people built their boats. We sized up same way with making sleds or canoes or boats. Just go look at another boat and copy that. We whip-sawed the lumber and plane it with a jack plane. I built three or four boats up there at Sulatna.

We let our lumber dry and very little cotton I used. I didn't have to use much cotton because I season my lumber before I built. And we have boat clamps. Clamp, nail, and move ahead. We use two clamps. There's quite a bit to that. I can't explain. Anyway I watched other boats being built, how they are built and everything and copied it. I never had to bail water hardly.

One spring especially I remember I came down down on a raft. We went out in the spring of the year with dog team. Me and a fellow named Edward Clarence. He told me that he knew all that country where I was going. That's before I bought the trapline up the Sulatna. I said, "If you know that country real well, how about going up with me and I'll buy all the groceries." He agreed in exchange for half the fur.

I thought he knew the country and he was worth it. But I

come to find out that he didn't know one lake. I had to hunt every lake and pack my canoe around the country. I still lived up to my promise and gave him half the fur but he wasn't worth it.

Charlie Carlo and his brother Frank came out to the river and met some boys camped about ten miles above us. They told them we were about ready to pull out with a raft. I had killed some caribou and dried them all. I saved my beaver meat and the castors too. Some traders wanted castors for five dollars a pound. I think they made perfume or something.

Charlie and Frank kept coming night and day to overtake us. They caught up before we got to the first canyon. My raft was double deck. Two layers of poles. I saw some beautiful fish wheel poles at the mouth of the Sulatna so I cut them down and made them into a deck. On the deck I built racks to hang up my beaver meat. In those days I was a working maniac. I'd sit down to skin beaver and find a good place up against a tree. My rifle on one side and my shotgun on the other. Anytime I heard a goose coming flying low, I'd shoot them right from where I'm sitting. When I get through skinning I pluck the goose. I had some rock salt to salt them down in a bucket. Here we have goose meat, fish, ducks, and beaver meat half dried. They taste better when they're half dried.

By the time Frank and Charlie came along in canoes they had nothing but beaver skins, their bedding, and a bottle of Tabasco sauce. Frank decided he wanted to stay on the raft. He was a good working fellow and knew the ways of the country. Charlie just wanted some grub and go on. He thought he would be way ahead of us.

We had a place to row on the raft and a little rule. Each man rowed for two hours then switch off. Every six or eight hours it would come around to our turn again. Then we picked up two trappers from Tanana, David Elia and George Yaska. We just kept coming night and day. We even had a stove aboard my raft ship.

That first night we saw Charlie Carlo's tent before we even got to the mouth of the Titna. Canvas pitched up and mosquito net. His brother said let's sneak by him. He was reading a book. But he heard us going by and before we were out of sight we saw him packing stuff down to his canoe.

He caught up to us before we got to the Titna and said he was ashamed to ask me if he could go along. He asked his brother, "No," he said, "you make your bed of roses now you have to go down in canoe." His own brother! Finally at the last minute I told him to tie up his canoe and come aboard. I didn't refuse anybody.

The raft was good because we could sleep on it. Just have to work a little to keep it out in the river. Moving night and day. Charlie or Frank would go ahead in their canoe two or three miles and cut dry timber. They split it and load it into their canoe. By the time we were in front of where he cut the wood he paddled out. That way we didn't even stop for stove wood. We came out in record time—four days and four nights.

Alaska Historical Library.

Ruby, photo taken by Clemons October 6, 1911.

Chapter Five: Blindness And Old Age

Going Blind

I discovered that I went blind through being reckless with DDT. I had a big fish camp up here three miles above Ruby. The flies were bad that summer. They were spoiling a lot of the fish we were putting up. I come into Ruby to Carl Bohn's store. I seen he had some gallon cans of DDT for killing mosquitoes or flies. I took some back to fish camp.

Like a damn fool I was. I didn't bother about reading the instructions. I just filled up the mosquito gun they called it, and sprayed it on the walls in the smokehouse. Gee, by next morning you could see about three or four inches thick of flies over the floor. And I was reckless in spraying the walls. I sprayed above me where I should have sprayed down. Then it wouldn't get in my eyes.

Outside of the camp I had a hole in the ground where I dumped my slop and garbage. I sprayed this hole. The next morning I seen dead birds in there. They start eating off that dump pile and they just lay there dead. Well, I didn't bother to read the directions. I

Ruby, June 1980.

62

was supposed to dilute it with water. I just sprayed it straight from the can. There was a lot of holler about DDT them days, but I didn't bother about listening. They finally took that DDT off the market. But it was too late for me.

I noticed that fall, I was rubbing my eyes. I went blind fast. I didn't know it was that DDT until I was blind about eight or ten years. The doctors tried to find out how in the heck I went blind. I thought it was drinking. I just took it for granted the first years that I was blind that it was all due to whiskey, bad homebrew. But them days we were drinking store whiskey. I quit making homebrew years before that. When we could buy whiskey in the store for a dollar and a half or two dollars a quart, it was cheaper to buy the whiskey. That was early '50's.

My partner, Robert Bob, got blind too. He got into trouble up here at Kokrines. Three or four young fellows were fighting and drinking whiskey. They kill one another off. My partner could only see with one eye a little when he cut his throat. Well, the doctors ask all kinds of questions about what I was doing and whether I lift heavy things. Do all kinds of tests. Finally I find out it was that DDT.

We were at fish camp every summer when I was going blind. It took almost two years to go blind. My daughters and sons helped me a lot. Any one of my sons would drive the boat, Billy or Allen or Harold. Morris McCarty and Patty was too young. I was fishing and trying to take care of the dogs. I watered them in the morning and evening before feeding time. But I was unable to see good.

One day I tried to water those dogs and, gee, I just missed the can. I couldn't

Bank on the Yukon at Ruby.

63

see the dogs or the dog pans anymore. I threw my hands in the air. The old woman was cutting fish along with two other women. I says to her, "I'm going to town. Damned if I can find the dogs anymore." I got Billy to drive the boat for me to Ruby.

I walked up to the welfare agent and I says, "I give in. I'll take an application for aid now. I was doing good, but this morning I finally threw my hands up in the air and says I'm going to quit."

She says, "It's about time." She was asking me to get a disability pension two or three years before that. I would say no, I don't need it yet. I was too proud of myself. I said as long as I can work I'm not going to receive any pension from the government.

After I got pension I tried it one more summer fishing. But the boys had to do most of the heavy work around the camp. I couldn't do any of the heavy work like I used to. So we discontinued the fish camp.

Our aid wasn't much those days. We was getting very little. Still, I never kicked. I was glad to get the few dollars extra in order to make a living. We started on forty or fifty dollars a month. Look what it is today, pretty near $500 and they're raising it yet. They treat old people pretty good nowadays.

In the old days we had to make a living till we die. We had to work. From what I seen of old people, they were out hunting, fishing and cutting steamboat wood. They'd go hunting. That's how old people made their living in this country. There was no such thing as old age pensions or social security.

Things changed since I went blind. We had no snow machines at the time I went blind. For transportation we had to hitch up our dogs. We had no chainsaws, we had to work the

Yrjana's warehouse in Ruby, 1980.

hard way with two man saws. I never used a chainsaw in my life. I can do pretty good with sawing wood now. I just stand in one place and have a pile of wood right close by, within reach. I can't do nothing where I have to go some distance. I can split some of my wood for a heater stove with a wedge and machine hammer. I can't split them fine but in half or quarter.

Since I went blind and lost my hearing I don't go around much. I very seldom go around and visit and listen to whatever the people is talking about. They have to yell right in my ear before I can hear anything. I used to listen to the news everyday, but I can't even hear that anymore since I lost my hearing. I'm old and I guess I don't give a darn anymore for the way that things turn out.

I don't know what would make it easier for a blind person. I been figuring on getting a seeing-eye dog for the last ten years·now. But I decided not to because I'll be walking through the streets and they'll get into a dog fight. I don't want to have my seeing-eye dog chewed up. Maybe in cities like Anchorage or Fairbanks it'll be better for a dog. Long ago I watched a fellow in Fairbanks when I could see. I followed him all the way up Cushman Street just to see what that dog would do. When he wants to cross the street, he'd stop. He'd look up and down and when he sees it's all clear to go across, he'd tug. He'd lead his master across the street. Then he'd go to some business house like he knows where he's going.

I tell you, a lot of times I wish I could

Ruby community hall and city office, 1980.

65

see again. A lot of times I get someplace and I'm lost. I can walk a good road by myself. I walked up to the Ruby airport several times all alone. But I have a hard time going straight. I turn to the left or the right a little bit and somebody have to correct me. I'm used to walking with someone holding on to my arm or hand, like my grandkids, Allen, Joey, or any one of Clara's daughters. They lead me around town to the store or post office.

When I go to Fairbanks I can't stand around the streets for all the cars and everything going by. When I go in there it's generally for medical attention. I stayed at the hospital once and once I stayed at Careage North. Gee whiz, I came away from there batty.

Careage North gets on your nerves. I was there for eight days. People howling all night. Especially an old woman. I was there in the summer and one day there was thunder and lightning or something hit their power plant. All the lights went out. All of a sudden people start yelling the end of the world is coming now. Somebody would start crying. I'd say, "Well, let it come. We can't stop it." All night long while I'm laying awake there somebody groaning. It just got on my nerves. When I got out of there I was acting crazy. I wasn't myself.

I don't want to go back to Careage North now. I told one of my daughters to make appointment at the Pioneer's home. I think it's quieter there and I know a lot of people there. I don't think I'd have any trouble getting admitted because I've worked with the pioneers. And they're taking anybody now, full Athabaskans. My aid and social security would take care of me as far as board is concerned. But my kids wouldn't send me up there. They'd rather take care of me.

Chapter Six: I Learned From My Dad

Clara Honea is Billy McCarty, Sr.'s oldest daughter. Chapter Six is a collection of some memories and thoughts of her dad in her own words.

He Really Loved Me

I wanted to add some things to my father's book that he wouldn't talk about very much himself. Especially a lot of the things that he did for us when we were kids. I remember when he used to go out hunting. He always took me along. While we were sitting around the campfire he talked to me. He'd tell me not to drink or smoke when I grew up, not to use too much makeup or I'd look cheap. He told me always to be honest and people would respect me. I observed how he made his deals with men he trapped with. At the end of their trapping I saw that he divided money with them evenly. When he told me to be honest I know that he lived by it. That was real important to me.

I remember the times he used to come to Kokrines after the end of the fur trapping season. He would bring me a big bundle of weasle skins. At that time the only thing it meant to me was the two or three dollars that it was going to bring when I sold them. I thought that was really big money. I could buy candy bars! Now when I think back I know he really loved me to take the time to skin those weasles and stretch them and bring them into Kokrines for me.

We were out in spring camp when I was just a little girl. He'd make whistles for me then out of young willow trees and

Clara Honea Collection.

Don and Clara Honea in front of the old Ruby store, 1956.

little boats with the cottonwood bark. I liked that, those were really special. Every year he'd make them for me, till I was 13 years old.

He really worked hard for us. When we lived at Mouse Point he used to go in the hills there and be gone about four hours. He'd come home with gas can full of currants, blueberries, or raspberries. Mom would make jelly or jam out of that all day, and store it for the winter. And he would hunt for duck and geese, salt them down in barrels in the fall the way some people do with fish now. I remember the best meals ever, Thanksgiving or Christmas. Mom used to soak those salted geese and make delicious roast, mashed potatoes from the garden and relish from the berries they put away. Those were really the best meals. I can't forget them. On holidays when I'm cooking, I think about those dinners and wish for them.

Springtime

Wintertime Dad used to go thirty miles up the Novi trapping. He'd always get a big supply of grub in the falltime. You probably wondered why he said that he always bought two outfits. That's because he'd leave a big outfit with Mom and the kids in Kokrines so we could go to school. He would take an outfit up the Novi. Since I was the oldest he would take me out with him sometimes, hunting and trapping until Billy Jr. was old enough.

Till I was thirteen years old I always used to go hunting with him in canoe. We'd go to the lakes along the Novi. When it's time to go home we'd walk through the portage to the river and he'd tell me to get in there first while he holds the canoe. I used to be really scared because the Novi River is swift and there'd be banking. I always thought that piece of bank sloping over the river would fall over.

Clara Honea cutting fish in Ruby, 1962.

A whole bunch of people went to spring camp up the Novi. It took about a week to come down, maybe a little longer if people are visiting one another, or stop for fishing. People used to tie their boats or raft to one another and visit while they go down river. Usually it took us two weeks because Dad had to stop at every good fishing and hunting place while all the others headed for town. I used to wish we could rush into town with the others. That was fun. People used to start shooting when the rafts were about four or five miles up river from Kokrines. Then the people that were in town would welcome us and shoot back.

It always used to be so much fun to get back to town in the springtime. People start putting in their gardens and getting ready for fish camps. Lots of times we were one of the first ones to head for fish camp and that was so lonesome because everybody was in town then. There was lots of good things going on in town. But Dad wanted to start fishing early so he'd move his family to fish camp around the middle of June to Mouse Point which was seven miles above Kokrines. That's where we used to fish before we moved to Ruby in '48.

Clara Honea: "This picture is of a whole bunch of people that went to spring camp up the Novi and are coming down now. Somewhere along the way we caught up to them and now Dad is towing the whole works. Our boat is in the middle. You can see some people sitting around. They're having a big gambling game. This might be 1944, the last time we went camping up the Novi."

Old Pioneer Hall in Ruby, 1980.

69

An Important Influence

Mom and Dad were an important influence on us. Mom never said much but she was always home and lived her life in such a way that set an example for her children to follow. She always said, when someone be mean or say bad things about us, to let it go, never fight back or defend ourself. We were to be kind to them instead and see only the good things in others.

They always told us to share food, even if it's our last. Never let anyone leave our home without a meal. Never make bad feelings over food, because food comes along every day. Whenever Dad got a moose, they gave most of it away. They always shared, though they had a big family to feed. I tell all my kids that now. I tell them to feed anyone who comes to our home. Especially when people come for spring carnival, and whether they're drunk or not, to feed them anyway.

Dad was always the chief or leader. When the school teachers had a problem, or needed advice, they went to him. And he was a doctor-like in Kokrines. When someone got hurt they would come to our house and get my dad to help them. Even three or four o'clock in the morning somebody would knock and I knew somebody got hurt. My dad would rush out and help them. He never complained.

I'm the same way, I guess I learned that from him, also. He had a real good doctor book that I always studied when I was growing up. There was never comics, True Stories, or any junk to read then. We only had this doctor book and I read it from cover to cover. I still abide by a lot of the stuff I learned from

70

that doctor book. When he helped people it was before health aides. He even sewed up one missionary's hand. He sewed it with plain needle and thread. It healed real good.

Good To Us

A lot of the stories Dad told here in his book, I remember. Ever since I was a little girl he'd tell them off and on. One of my favorite stories of Dad's is about when he was coming down the Koyukuk River in spring. He couldn't forget Mom, she was so beautiful. He was going down the river to Kokrines to visit her. He finished with hunting rats up around Huslia or Allakaket or somewhere. The water was high. He was in his canoe looking at Mom's picture, thinking about her so hard that he wasn't looking where he was going. He hit a snag and tipped over, almost drowned.

When he talked about his dad in this book I thought, now I understand why he was so good to us and why his family was so important. I think he was really hurt by his father. He really did work hard all his life and took care of us and gave us advice. We were a big family and he and Mom taught us how to share and do things together. From time to time I write letters to him and tell him about it, that I'm glad he was so strict with us and thank him for all he did for us. Now I know that he loved us. Back then I couldn't understand it. I thought, Oh, he's just mean. Now I'm really glad I had him for a father.

Ruby, looking up the Yukon River, 1980.

71

Index